My Feelings

FEAR

Published by Creative Education
123 South Broad Street
Mankato, Minnesota 56001

Creative Education is an imprint of
THE CREATIVE COMPANY.

Design and production by EVANSDAY DESIGN

My Feelings

EAR

LENORE FRANZEN

LIBRARY OF CONGRESS CATALOGING-IN-PUBLICATION DATA
Franzen, Lenore.
Fear / by Lenore Franzen.
p. cm. — (My feelings)
Includes bibliographical references and index.
ISBN 1-58341-319-7
1. Fear—Juvenile literature. I. Title.

BF575.F2F73 2004
152.4'6—dc22   2004049336

First Edition
9 8 7 6 5 4 3 2 1

PHOTOGRAPHS BY: Corbis (Brian Bailey, Jamie Budge, DiMaggio/Kalish, Flash 90/Reuters
Newmedia Inc., Layne Kennedy, Mark M. Lawrence, Lewis Alan/Corbis Sygma, John Madere,
O'Brien Productions, Denis O'Regan, Eric Perlman, David Raymer, Reuters, Lynda Richardson,
Norbert Schaefer, Ariel Skelley, A & J Verkaik, Bob Winsett, David Zimmerman)

FEELING

A

4

RAID

A person who has a fear of high places has acrophobia (ak-roh-FOH-be-uh).

People feel many different things. They can feel happy, mad, sad, or afraid. These feelings are called emotions. Fear is an emotion. When you feel fear, you feel afraid.

Most of the time, fear helps keep you safe. Fear tells you to pull away from something hot. Or not to climb too high. Fear tells you to stay away from barking dogs and hissing cats.

Too much fear can be bad for you. Strong fears are called phobias. A phobia may keep you from learning new things. Or making new friends.

A person who is afraid a lot
may be called a *chicken*
or *scaredy cat.*

ons

?

WHAT

S

SC

8

RES

YOU?

Thunder, wind, or the boom of fireworks can make you feel afraid. Ghost stories, nightmares, or imaginary creatures can be scary. Many people are afraid of the dark. Others are afraid of bugs or snakes.

Many people are scared of things they have never tried. Climbing a tree for the first time can be scary because you might fall. The first day of school scares some kids. So does moving to a new neighborhood or going to the doctor.

You may also be afraid of things you cannot change. Being in an accident can make you feel scared. Listening to grown-ups fight can be scary, too. You may be afraid when someone you love gets sick.

A terrorist is someone who
tries to control people by
scaring them.

F

AR

Two things that many kids fear are
bullies and making mistakes.

When you are scared, your brain sends a special message to your body. Sometimes, this message tells you to face the danger. Other times, it tells you to run away.

When your body feels fear, your heart pounds, and your muscles tighten. You breathe fast. Your whole body may shake. You may sweat. You may have to go to the bathroom. Fear can even make you sick.

When you are scared, you may cover your face with your hands. Or hide under a blanket. Or cry. You may pull back, just as a turtle hides in its shell.

musc

} The fear of being in front of a group of people is called stage fright.

F

16

A scared dog flattens its ears back, drops its tail, and lowers its body.

Most people try to stay away from things they fear. They do not watch scary movies or TV shows. They do not read stories that scare them. They stay away from people who are mean. They do not go into dark places.

Everyone feels fear sometimes. It is okay to say you are afraid. One of the best ways to feel better is to talk to someone. Tell that person what makes you afraid. Ask questions about the things that scare you. That will help the fear go away.

19

NAME THAT FEAR

Many things can cause fear. See if you can name them!

What You Need

NOTECARDS

A PENCIL

ONE GROWN-UP AND FIVE KIDS

What You Do

1. Ask a grown-up to help you write something scary on each card (for example, the dark, thunder, bullies, snakes, ghosts, spiders, monsters).

2. Turn the cards upside down and mix them up.

3. Taking turns, pick a card and act it out. Stop when someone guesses right.

4. Have each person tell a good way to make the fear go away.

WORDS TO KNOW

emotions feelings; happiness and sadness are kinds of emotions

imaginary creatures things that are not real, such as monsters

muscles parts of the body that help you move

phobias very strong feelings of fear about something, such as water, spiders, or high places

READ MORE
EXPLORE THE WEB

Hoban, Russell. *Bedtime for Frances*. San Francisco: Harper Trophy, 1995.

Mayer, Mercer. *There's a Nightmare in My Closet*. New York: E. P. Dutton, 1992.

Roca, Nuria. *Scared: From Fear to Courage*. Hauppauge, N.Y.: Barron's Educational Series, 2002.

Scott, Ann Herbert. *Brave as a Mountain Lion*. New York: Clarion Books, 1996.

AMERICA'S CHILDREN: BOOKS ABOUT FEARS

http://www.pampetty.com/fears.htm

KIDSHEALTH: BEING AFRAID

http://www.kidshealth.org/kid/feeling/emotion/afraid.html

INDEX